INVITATION TO MEDITATION

INVITATION
TO
MEDITATION

how to find peace
wherever you are

Howard Cohn

Foreword by Jack Kornfield

CHRONICLE BOOKS
SAN FRANCISCO

Text copyright © 2016 by Howard Cohn.

Foreword copyright © 2016 by Jack Kornfield.

All rights reserved. No part of this book may be reproduced in
any form without written permission from the publisher.

Library of Congress Cataloging-in-Publication Data available.

ISBN 978-1-4521-4434-4

Manufactured in China

Design by Tonje Vetleseter

10 9 8 7 6 5 4

Chronicle books and gifts are available at special quantity
discounts to corporations, professional associations, literacy
programs, and other organizations. For details and discount
information, please contact our corporate/premiums
department at corporatesales@chroniclebooks.com or at
1-800-759-0190.

Chronicle Books LLC
680 Second Street
San Francisco, California 94107
www.chroniclebooks.com

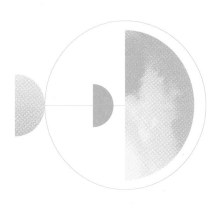

FOREWORD

This book is a treasure you can hold in your cupped hands. The simple and elegant teachings within these pages bring you back to a quiet mind and an open heart. They remind you to be alive and awake here, in the reality of the present moment.

Howie has been a dear friend and colleague of mine for decades, and his teachings always inspire me. They offer the immediacy and freshness of what is known in the Zen tradition as "beginner's mind"— that is, a state of openness to possibility and insights. They give a deep practical understanding of how to learn the revolutionary art of mindful presence.

Howie's teachings are at once simple and profound. He points to the nature of the mind itself. Read this book closely, for these words can bring you to the essence of liberation of the heart, and the timeless freedom of spirit that is the birthright of us all. *Howie reminds you that what you seek is who you really are.* If this is hard to understand at first, hold it as a powerful koan, or puzzle, to solve.

Take your time with these pages. Savor them like a cup of the finest tea.

Explore, listen, and learn with Howie how to live with an open mind and tender heart.

May these teachings bring you joy and great blessings.

Jack Kornfield
Spirit Rock Center, 2015

Invitation to Meditation

Imagine feeling calm and content wherever you are. Imagine feeling that your life is so complete—right here, right now—that you do not wish to be anywhere else.

Imagine feeling this way even when your to-do list is overflowing. You are unrushed and free of anxiety. You are able to act intelligently, skillfully, and swiftly, with clarity and ease. You feel inexhaustibly alive and aware.

Imagine feeling this way in an airport or shopping mall, or even in rush-hour traffic. Your surroundings might be chaotic, but inside you feel a sense of stillness and peace.

Imagine feeling this way when you are alone. You are enjoying solitude, immersed in the life that is inside and around you. Your senses are wide awake. Sights are vivid, sounds clear, tastes and smells rich and alive.

You are open to your thoughts and feelings—
you are not resisting them and not bothered
by them. They pass through your mind like
clouds drifting through an empty sky.

Imagine feeling this way while in the company of others. You feel strong and steady, not reactive to criticism. You are praised for something, and then blamed for something, and yet you maintain your equilibrium as you experience one and then the other— a windfall and then a loss, success and then failure, exquisite pleasure and then uncomfortable pain. From one to the other, you are calm and balanced.

You are riding the waves of your life, not drowning in them.

You need not just imagine feeling so whole, so full, so intimately in touch with your life. You can feel this way *right now* by stepping out of your imagination and embracing reality, just as it is, just as you are.

But don't just believe me—see for yourself.

I invite you to a place where love, compassion, and creativity abound.

I invite you to see that inner peace is nearer— and easier to experience—than you think.

I invite you to the present moment.

"The present moment." You're hearing this expression a lot these days. But what exactly is the present moment? It's the place I've just described—the place of calm and ease. But it's also the place of relentless deadlines and to-do lists, of car repairs and tax returns, of regrets and disappointments, and the myriad other anxieties and sorrows that accompany human existence.

How can the two places possibly be the same?

Well, consider how many of your anxieties stem from events in the future. And then consider that the future is not part of the present moment. The future hasn't happened yet. You can only *imagine* the future. It's not real.

And consider that your regrets and disappointments—such as that failed relationship, that job you lost, or that comment you wish you hadn't made—stem from events that have already happened. Whether they happened last year, last month, or in the last hour, these events are in the past. And the past has passed. The past is not part of the present moment. Those events are now memories, and memories live in your imagination. You can only *imagine* the past. It's not real.

Perhaps you can see now that the past and future are actually imaginary. They are not real. They are real in the sense that you did experience the past and you will experience the future, but they're not real in the sense that they are not happening now. They are not part of the present moment. And yet we spend so much time each day lost in thoughts of our past and future—lost in imaginings of where we think we came from, where we think we're going, and who we think we are. In truth, these imaginings are just that—they are imaginary.

What a joy, to wake up to the simple reality of the present moment.

So, if the past and future are imaginary, and if so much of what we believe about ourselves is imaginary, what is real?

The present moment is real. You can experience the present moment simply by opening up your five senses to the world around you. Try it right now. See, feel, hear, smell, and taste what's real in this moment.

See the words on this page—they're real. Look around and see the sights all around you—the pictures on the wall, the flowers in the vase, the reflections of light dancing throughout the room—these are real.

Feel this book in your hands—it's real. The weight of it, its textures pressing against your fingertips—they're real. Feel, too, the ground beneath your feet—it's real. The sensation of standing or sitting—that is, the feel of the seat and floor beneath you, the feel of your shirt against your skin, the feel of your belt around your waist—these sensations are real.

Hear the sounds around you—the rustle of wind through the trees, the beep of a phone, the honk of a car, or the buzz of silence— they're real.

Smell the fragrances in your immediate environment—the lingering scent of soap on your hands, the aroma of something cooking in the oven, or the bouquet of city smells coming through an open window— they're real.

Tastes, too—the hint of toothpaste, the aftertaste of coffee, or the delicious blandness of a clean, empty palate—they're real.

We know these are real because we experience them with our five bodily senses: our senses of sight, touch, sound, smell, and taste. These sensory experiences prove undeniably that we are alive—that we are here in the present moment.

When we notice what we are experiencing with our five senses, we know that we are experiencing the present moment.

In addition to these sensory experiences, we also experience our breath in the present moment. Our breath is real. As we breathe, we draw air into and out of our lungs, and oxygen circulates through our living, pulsating body. Our experience of our breath proves undeniably that we are alive—that we are here in the present moment.

When we notice our breathing, we know that we are experiencing the present moment.

And, in addition to our sensory experiences and our breath, we also experience our thoughts in the present moment. Notice what's on your mind right now, just as you notice what you can see and hear with your eyes and ears. Our experience of our thoughts is as real as our experiences of the five senses and our breathing. Our experience of our thoughts proves undeniably that we are alive—that we are here in the present moment.

And the simple act of noticing our thoughts frees us from our attachment to them, frees us from being defined by them, frees us from the control they can have over us and the emotional turmoil that can result from being controlled by them.

When we notice our thoughts, we are able to acknowledge that they are just thoughts, and we know that we are experiencing the present moment.

But don't just believe me. See for yourself. Experience the present moment by, once again, opening up your five senses to the world around you. Notice what you see, feel, hear, smell, and taste in this present moment. Notice that you are breathing. Take a deep breath, and notice how air enters your body as you inhale, and how it leaves your body as you exhale. Notice what thoughts are floating through your mind. Don't judge them. Don't resist them. Simply notice them. Simply notice what it is to be alive.

For that's what you are when you're in the present moment: You are alive. Alive to the present, not trapped in the past. Alive to the present, not afraid of the future. Alive as your essential self, your true being, not bonded to the imaginary "me" that you think you are or hope to be. Alive to the vividness of life—not lost in your imagination, not missing the exquisite beauty of the world around you.

And when you are in the present moment, you are free. Free from the past, free from the future. Free from expectations, free from judgments. Free from the tangle of preoccupations of the distracted mind. Free from the endless complications that exist in the realm of your imagination. Free to awaken, to open, to tap into the happiness that is within you always—the happiness that is your true nature. Free to be just as you are. Free to just *be*.

Try it again. Open up your five senses and sink more deeply into your body's experience. Take another breath, and again simply notice. Not reaching. Not resisting. Not judging. Just noticing. Just being.

You have arrived.

Welcome to the present moment.

Wow. It's nice here, you think. How can I stay? How can I feel this way—this ease, this spaciousness, this calm—more often? You may feel it slipping away right this very minute and think, How do I return to the present moment?

In reality, you never leave the present moment. You're *always* here. You're never *not* here. You only *imagine* that you leave the present moment.

You are anchored to the present moment in three different ways. One, by your body, which contains the five senses. Whenever you feel as if you've slipped away from the present moment, allow each of the senses to reconnect with your immediate sur-roundings. Allow yourself to be immersed in the sights, textures, sounds, scents, and tastes of the present moment. As you do so—again, by simply noticing—you are aware that you are alive in the present moment.

Two, you are anchored here by your breath. With each inhale, and with each exhale, you sink more deeply into the present moment. Inhaling, you expand. Exhaling, you release. Inhaling, you experience the breath. Exhaling, you let it go. Inhaling, you settle into the body's natural stillness. Exhaling, you gently harmonize your body and mind. Inhaling and exhaling, you are aware that you are alive in the present moment.

Three, you are anchored here by your awareness of your thoughts. Notice them as you would notice the sights and sounds around you. Notice them as you would notice a cloud passing through the sky. Notice that certain emotions may arise with certain thoughts. Don't stop them. Don't be afraid of them. Don't react to them. Just notice them. Let them come and go like changing weather patterns. And in doing so, may you realize that they are just thoughts and emotions—nothing more. And in doing so, may you realize that you are still here—still anchored in the present moment.

By now you realize that you never actually leave the present moment. You only imagine that you do. You seem to leave the present moment, quite simply, when your mind wanders away from it. The term "wandering mind" is commonly heard and easy enough to understand. But let's look at it more closely, because herein lies the golden key to staying in the present moment.

How exactly does our mind wander?

Our mind wanders when we don't notice our thinking; that is, when we loosen our awareness and allow our thoughts to become more than just thoughts. We allow them to connect, one by one, like the links of a chain, and we mindlessly follow after them. We then become lost in thought. Whether lost in pleasant thoughts or unpleasant thoughts, we are nevertheless lost. We are no longer present. Our bodies become tense as our thinking mind gives way to our imagination. We abandon the present moment for a fantasy world of memories, anticipation, hopes, worries, and regrets. We abandon the real experience of our natural self— the living, breathing creature of the present moment—for our imagined self. Our imagined self is the person we *think* we are—that imaginary character of our past and future, that character from the stories we create about ourselves in our mind.

Let's see this in action.

A businessman gathering papers for a work assignment begins thinking about a mistake he made recently at the office. He replays the episode in his mind, reliving the embarrassment. He begins to worry that he will repeat the mistake which could cause him to lose his job. He imagines it happening—his boss leaning forward in his chair to deliver the bad news that he is no longer needed at the company. He imagines packing up his things at his desk. He imagines telling his friends that he was fired, and he cringes at the thought of their reactions. He imagines becoming destitute, and his body is gripped with fear. He is no longer present; he is lost in thought.

A woman is cooking dinner when she suddenly thinks of her mother. Her mother, whom she has never thanked for the sacrifices she made for the family over the years. Her mother, whom she imagines to be sad and lonely. Her mother, who will need assistance one day but who doesn't like asking for help and will surely make things difficult. Weighed down by these imaginings, her belly now twisted with worry, the woman cooking dinner is no longer hungry.

A young man is happily packing a suitcase, looking forward to a weekend vacation. As he folds his clothes, he dreamily imagines arriving at his hotel, stepping into the tropical sunlight, and listening to music by the seashore. Continuing to pack, his body tenses in a state of restless anticipation. He can't wait—he wants to be there *now*. Everything will be perfect, he thinks.

It can happen in an instant. Faster than the speed of light, we seem to travel from the present moment to the far-flung corners of our imagination. When we are lost in thought, playing out scenarios in our minds as these three characters are doing, our bodies feel the physical impact as if the scenarios were really happening. Our chest tightens, we feel nervous flutterings in our torso, our breath shortens. But these scenarios are not real—they are imagined. What unnecessary stress we put on our bodies by giving in to the wandering mind.

Fortunately, we can return to the present moment just as quickly as we seem to have left it by noticing that our mind has wandered and accessing the sensations of the five senses. The fearful businessman need only feel the textures of the papers in his hand to return with full focus to the project he's working on. The woman worried about her mother need only inhale the aromas of her cooking to return to the delicious moment before her. The young man restlessly anticipating his vacation need only breathe deeply and recognize that perfection lies not in the future but is right here, right now.

And, just like that, each of them returns to the present moment. Just like that, they cut through the chain of delusion—that ever-lengthening chain of connected thoughts and associations that, one by one, seemed to lead them away from the present moment and deep into their imagination. Fully present once again, their bodies relax. Their minds clear. They re-awaken to the miracles before them. They reawaken to the present moment.

When you read about the young man packing for vacation, you might have been thinking, Who doesn't enjoy looking forward to the weekend? Or, What's wrong with a feeling of happy anticipation?

Being lost in thought is not always the unpleasant experience of the fearful business-man or the worried daughter. Being lost in thought is surely enjoyable to the young man looking forward to his vacation. Nevertheless, when we are lost in thought—be it a happy or unhappy thought—we are not here. We are living in our imagination. We are missing out on the magically unfolding present moment. We are depriving ourselves of the richly textured, full-body experience of being alive.

You're still thinking of that young man and his vacation, aren't you? You're wondering why anyone should want to avoid feeling that kind of happiness. But consider that what he's feeling isn't a state of true happiness. It's a state of suspended happiness. It's the happiness of *if only*. If only the weekend would arrive, everything would be perfect.

Consider the other "if only" scenarios in our lives. If only I could solve this problem. If only I could meet this goal. If only he or she loved me. If only I could make that purchase. If only I were more like him or her.

The imagined happiness and security we feel when we think of fulfilling our hopes and desires is just that: imaginary. It's a happiness that is dependent on specific circumstances. It's a happiness that we gain when circumstances are in our favor, and a happiness that we lose when those circumstances change.

.

This "happiness" is actually a form
of bondage.

True happiness is free—no strings attached.

True happiness is real.

True happiness is here and now.

True happiness is lasting.

True happiness is peace.

True happiness is our true nature, our natural state, and our birthright.

True happiness is *all there is*.

Why would we ever choose anything else?

But we do. We enslave ourselves to ever-changing circumstances and outcomes. We tie our happiness, our well-being, and our enjoyment of this most precious gift of life to the unpredictable whims of the world. We seek happiness outside ourselves when there is an abundance within. Why? Why do we do this to ourselves?

Perhaps we know of no other way. Perhaps because it is our *mind's habit* to wander— to become lost in thought, swept up in imagined scenarios, and attached to outcomes.

There *is* another way.

That way is here in the present moment. That way is found by guiding our attention back to the present moment when it wanders away from it. Gently. And repeatedly. That way is found by reconnecting with our breath and our bodily experience—sights, sounds, and sensations—again and again. That way is found by establishing *new habits* of mind.

And how can we do that?

We can meditate.

Meditation is the training of our minds to dwell more fully and frequently in the present moment. It is an act that we can practice—much as one practices the piano or a foreign language—in order to strengthen our skills in experiencing and staying in the present moment. In doing so, we quiet our minds and relax our bodies; we more easily tap into the natural happiness, peace, and ease that is within us; and we lessen the desire to be anywhere other than right where we are.

If that sounds too complicated, consider this: Meditation is as simple as noticing what you are experiencing and what you are thinking.

Meditation is as simple as noticing that your mind has wandered, and then noticing that it has returned to the present moment.

Meditation is as simple as noticing your emotions as you feel them—not trying to change them, but just noticing them. It's as simple as sitting quietly. It's as simple as observing the rise and fall of your breath as you inhale and exhale.

Still not convinced that you can meditate?
Or does it sound too easy to be true?

Then see for yourself. Right now, see what it's like to meditate.

Find a place of quiet and take a seat in a chair or on the floor. Sit upright in a way that's comfortable—not so comfortable that you will become drowsy, but comfortable enough to sustain the seated position for an extended period of time. If you're sitting in a chair, you can have your feet flat against the floor, your rear on the seat of the chair, and your back erect but relaxed. If you're sitting on the floor, you can place a cushion beneath you, or sit directly on the floor's firm surface. You can sit in a cross-legged or kneeling position. You can let your arms hang by your sides or let your hands rest in your lap. Once you find yourself in a relaxed seated position, turn this page.

Now, don't do anything.

For once in your life, *don't do anything.*

How does it feel?

Notice. Just notice.

Notice how effortless it is just to notice.

Notice what you're experiencing with your five senses. Start by noticing that you're sitting. How exactly do you notice that you're sitting? You feel the sensation of your rear against the surface of whatever you're sitting on, and the points of contact your feet are making with the floor.

Now notice the sounds all around you—
the ticking of a clock, or the muffled traffic
out the window. Notice the smells. Notice
the tastes, and the presence of your tongue
nestled within your mouth. Just notice.

Notice the sensations of your whole body in this sitting posture. Feel the aliveness of your body—that is, its living, pulsing quality. Simply experience what it is to be alive.

Now turn your attention to your breathing.
Just notice it.

Notice that some breaths are long. Some are short. Some are rough and some are smooth, some deep and some shallow. Make no effort to alter your breath. Instead, simply notice it, just as it is. As you breathe in, feel the gentle rise of your chest and belly as air enters your body. As you breathe out, feel the fall of your chest and belly as air leaves your body. As you breathe in and out, feel the sensations of air flowing gently through your nostrils and into and out of your lungs. Focus on these sensations. Connect to them. Sink into them, and experience—truly experience—what it is to simply breathe.

Continue breathing, noticing, and savoring,
one breath at a time.

Reading this sentence, breathe in.

Reading this sentence, breathe out.

Reading this one, breathe in.

Reading this one, breathe out.

This one, in.

This one, out.

And continue on your own. No need to be concerned about the breath that has just occurred; it has come and gone. Notice just *this* breath.

And now *this* breath.

And now *this* breath.

Continue allowing your body to breathe naturally. To breathe by itself. Then, when your eyes arrive at the end of this sentence, close them, take a few breaths, and notice the natural stillness that you experience simply by closing your eyes and breathing.

You may have heard sounds while your eyes were closed. You may hear sounds now—sounds in your immediate environment, distant sounds, or even what might be called the sounds of silence. These sounds may draw your attention away from your breathing. This is natural. Let these sounds be heard. Let all sounds, loud and soft, be heard without naming them or judging them. Simply notice them, and then guide your attention back to your breathing.

Sensations, too, may arise that draw your attention away from your breath—sensations that you might typically overlook if you weren't paying attention, such as the feeling of your clothes against your skin, or tinglings of pressure here and there throughout your body. This is natural. Let these sensations be felt without analyzing them or judging them. Simply notice them, and then guide your attention back to your breathing.

Moods and emotions may arise as well. You may become annoyed or frustrated, bored or tired, excited or fearful, happy or elated. Don't try to stop these emotions or change them. Just notice them. They are natural— after all, you are alive. Let these moods and emotions be experienced without judgment, worry, or attachment. Just notice them. Let them come and let them go, and then guide your attention back to your breathing.

Thoughts, too, will inevitably arise. Thoughts
of to-do lists and deadlines, thoughts of
friendships and hobbies, thoughts of memories,
worries, and plans. Don't try to shut
out these thoughts. Don't judge them or
be afraid of them. Just notice them and
accept them as a natural expression of the
thinking human mind. Notice, simply, that
thoughts arise, and notice that they pass
by. Notice how they seem to connect to
each other—how one thought can lead to
another and then another, which causes
your mind to start wandering away. Notice
this, and then gently guide your attention
back to your breathing.

Inevitably, more thoughts will arise. Simply notice them, and again guide your attention back to your breathing.

And again, inevitably, *more* thoughts will arise. Simply notice them, and again guide your attention back to your breathing.

This is meditation.

When we meditate, our minds are like the sky: vast, welcoming, and open to all experiences. Nothing needs to be done, and nothing needs to be undone. We neither embellish our experience nor do we try to suppress it. We simply notice it. We accept it. And we refocus our attention, again and again. In doing so, we break the mind's habit of becoming lost in thought. We break the mind's habit of leaping into imagined scenarios. We become more accustomed to living—and more skilled at returning to—life in the present moment. We become more aware that we are alive; that we are here; that we are living and breathing in the present moment.

We realize that every moment is a new beginning—that we can always begin again.

After meditating a few times, you might find that you want to start a so-called "meditation practice."

A practice, by definition, is an act that is performed over and over for the purpose of strengthening a skill. One practices piano to strengthen the ability to play music. One practices a foreign language to strengthen fluency in another tongue. One practices meditation to strengthen the ability to stay in the present moment.

The key organ involved in meditation is the mind. Sometimes known as the thinking muscle, the mind is capable of such miraculous feats—among countless other things, it processes information, houses our memories, and enables us to experience our whole sensory universe—that it's easy to overlook the fact that we can exercise and train it just as we can many other muscles in the body. In a meditation practice, we train our minds to stay in the present moment. We do this by constantly guiding our attention back to the present moment during a meditation session, and by meditating on a regular basis, be it once a day, once a week, or as often as we choose.

If you're thinking, Who has time for that?, this is a sign that carving out some time for meditation is just what you need.

With practice, your mind will become more and more used to staying in the present moment. With practice, it will become a habit—a healthy habit that breaks the unhealthy habits of the wandering mind. With practice, you'll get used to sitting still and accessing the natural calm that is within you. You'll stop trying to go somewhere else—whether your current habit is retreating to memories of the past or incessant planning for the future—and you'll start enjoying being right where you are.

You'll embrace your natural state—that of a *human being,* not a *human doing.*

Meditate once and you will likely feel relaxed right away. You may experience beginner's euphoria—a feeling of "That was easy!" or an instant connection to the present moment—or you may feel nervous, discouraged, or even more scatterbrained than before. In either case, try not to get attached to the results. Simply try it again. And again.

Meditate every day for a week and you will feel calmer, more present, and better equipped to ride the roller coaster of your life. You will become more aware of your habits—the healthy and unhealthy ones—and you will want to continue getting to know yourself better. You will have a greater intimacy with the present moment, and it will show in your interactions with the world around you.

Meditate every day for a year and you will not want to stop. You will be living life with mindfulness and compassion toward yourself and others. Your body and mind will be quieter and more relaxed. You will be more balanced and less reactive. You will realize that while you cannot escape the struggles in life, you can meet them with a sense of presence and confidently proceed with whatever actions are called for. To-do lists will overflow, but you will complete each item with focus and clarity. Loss and misfortune will befall you, but you will receive them with calm and groundedness. Relationships will have their ups and downs, but you will ride the waves with patience and understanding. Fearful thoughts will creep into your mind, but you will not let them take root and control you; instead you will acknowledge that they are just thoughts and let them pass by. You will accept yourself. You will be happier.

You will know the difference between a
trained mind and an untrained mind.

An untrained mind is lost in thought.
A trained mind is focused.

An untrained mind goes where it wants.
A trained mind stays connected to what
is really happening.

An untrained mind is defensive, self-
conscious, and overprotective. A trained
mind is welcoming to new experiences.

An untrained mind is often agitated and worried. A trained mind is peaceful, calm, and steady.

An untrained mind is exhausted by its circuitous wanderings. A trained mind is active and wide awake.

An untrained mind is cluttered. A trained mind is spacious and clear-thinking.

An untrained mind is shackled to outcomes and circumstances. A trained mind is liberated and in search of adventure.

An untrained mind is uninspired. A trained mind is creative, intuitive, wise, and intelligent.

An untrained mind is elsewhere. A trained mind is right here, right now.

Which do you want? The choice is yours.

But don't just believe me. See for yourself.

If you continue to explore meditation, you will learn that there are many different approaches to it. There are various spiritual and cultural traditions, and various types of meditation practices. But you need not commit to a specific one to invite meditation into your life.

Consider that the term "meditation" can apply to any activity or practice that enables you to stay connected to life in the present moment, or that harmonizes your mind and body.

Indeed, there are so many opportunities in daily life to plant the seeds of meditation and awaken the experience of natural happiness. All you have to do is bring a kind, interested, and relaxed attention to whatever you are doing in the present moment, be it working at your desk, washing dishes, even brushing your teeth. Whatever the task, feel the movements and micro-movements of your body. Witness your felt sensations. Notice your thoughts, moods, and emotions without judgment. And let your body breathe.

Meditation doesn't have to be a big under-taking. By simply being mindful of your thoughts and actions throughout the day, just one moment at a time, you can live in a state of meditative awareness, which is itself a form of meditation. The more frequently you do so, the more comfortable and skilled you will become at abiding in the present moment. The more you will undo the mind's habit of wanting to be somewhere else, even while engaging in mundane tasks. The more you will see that no task feels mundane when we do it meditatively—that the mundane is, in fact, *miraculous*.

That the ordinary is, in fact, *extraordinary*.

When you first opened this book and began reading, you were asked to imagine feeling calm and content wherever you are; to imagine feeling that your life is so complete—right here, right now—that you do not wish to be anywhere else.

If you've arrived at the end of this book, chances are you don't have to imagine. You know, now, how it feels to be in the present moment. You know that the richness of life can be experienced firsthand, and that the secondhand version of life that plays out in your imagination pales in comparison. You understand that meditation is a portal to the present moment—that by simply noticing your bodily sensations, breath, and thoughts, you access inner peace and mental clarity while calming the body and mind. You acknowledge that you have a choice in how you are affected by life's challenges. Will you give into the untrained mind, tying your happiness and well-being to the unpredictable whims of the world? Or will you be the master of your experience and choose to stay here in the present moment? Will you accept this invitation to meditation?

Remember, there *is* a better way.
But don't just believe me. See for yourself!

ACKNOWLEDGMENTS

First, deep bows of gratitude to my passionate, inspirational editor, Elizabeth Yarborough, with whom I conceived this book through conversations, meditation sessions, and exchanged thoughts and writings. Thanks also to Sara Golski, Tonje Vetleseter, Yolanda Cazares, Stephanie Wong, and the rest of the team at Chronicle Books.

This book would not exist without the help of so many who have shaped my life and supported me. Among them are Ram Dass, whose book *Be Here Now* inspired me and at whose retreat I met Stephen Levine, who first introduced me to insight (or vipassana) meditation in which most of my teachings are rooted; the great meditation master Dipa Ma, whose warmth and power of awakening carried me through extended meditation retreats; Ajahn Sumedho, the Seattle-born monk whose wisdom, accessible style, earthiness, and sense of humor strongly resonate with me; Sayadaw U Pandita, who, during retreats and interviews in Burma and the United States, helped me see life distilled to the bare simplicity of the present moment; and the Master H. W. L. Poonja, who helped me stop looking beyond the present moment for happiness and to experience the joy of freedom. I always hear his voice in my teaching. Christopher Titmuss, whose affirmation early in my career gave me confidence that I could be a teacher; Sharon Salzberg, who kindly let me tag along as an assistant in my early teaching years; my original colleagues at Spirit Rock Meditation Center, including James Baraz, Sylvia Boorstein, Anna Douglas, and Sharda Rogell; and the many communities that invite me to teach meditation, including Westcoast Dharma Society in Vancouver, Insight Meditation Houston, Mariposa Sangha in Austin, Regina Insight Meditation Community, Prescott Insight Meditation, Victoria Insight Meditation Society, Edmonton Vipassana, Open Door Sangha in Santa Barbara, and many others. Mission Dharma, the community I lead here in San Francisco, has shown me the importance of practicing together with others and allowed me to share my love of meditation week after week for more than thirty years.

My friends and mentors of more than thirty-five years, Joseph Goldstein and Jack Kornfield, have impacted me in countless ways. Jack, a master teacher and unceasing supporter who has given me so many opportunities to share my teachings—thank you. And Joseph, whose wisdom and inexhaustible love of

meditation have been a constant inspiration—
thank you.

And special thanks to my family: My beautiful,
intelligent, open-minded parents, Babe and Jerry Cohn,
who trusted me and never tried to coerce me into
any life direction. They encouraged me to follow my
heart, instincts, and interests. They gave me the love
of adventure which I have followed both inwardly and
outwardly.

Thanks to my late grandmother, Rose Blumkin,
whose example of hard work, compassion, and gener-
osity fills me with pride.

Thanks to my brother Barry and sister Claudia,
who protected me as a kid and love and support me
as an adult.

Thank-you to my wife, Annie—my best friend and
co-pilot for the last twenty-five years. She is my true
guru. She is a master at being able to laugh at herself.
She has taught me not to take myself too seriously.
She always takes the high road and is quick to forgive.

And finally, thanks to my newest guru, my daughter,
Molly. The privilege of watching her grow up has given
me such an appreciation for each person's individual
essence which I call "Mollyness."

Thank you all.